T0068094

DRESS—AND LIVE—FOR

SUCCESS

DRESS—AND LIVE—FOR
SUCCESS

Tips from a Florida Professional
That Will Benefit Any Man or Woman Who
Wants to Make a Lasting Impression

Colleen S. Craddock

DESIGNED FOR REALTORS – BANKERS
TV ANNOUNCERS – CORPORATE CEOs

PROFESSIONALS WHO DESIRE TO MAKE THEIR
FIRST IMPRESSION A LASTING IMPRESSION

iUniverse, Inc.
Bloomington

DRESS—AND LIVE—FOR SUCCESS
Tips from a Florida Professional That Will Benefit Any Man or Woman Who Wants to Make a Lasting Impression

iUniverse books may be ordered through booksellers or by contacting:

iUniverse
1663 Liberty Drive
Bloomington, IN 47403
www.iuniverse.com
1-800-Authors (1-800-288-4677)

ISBN: 978-1-4759-1491-7 (sc)
ISBN: 978-1-4759-1492-4 (e)

Printed in the United States of America

iUniverse rev. date: 04/24/2012

Contents

Acknowledgments

I dedicate this book to all the men and women who have achieved their professional goals, who have taken steps in their profession by being knowledgeable in their fields of expertise. They dress for their success and have an attitude of pride in their appearance and a positive outlook toward their future. These are the men and women who have set examples for the next generation.

I also want to thank the many realtors I have worked with who showed me the ropes and taught me what they know about how to become successful in this profession.

I cannot express enough thanks to my husband, Larry, who was a big help during my writing of this book. His belief in me, his encouragement, and his honest opinions gave me so much inspiration. He is my hero, my best friend, and my strongest supporter. Two of my very best friends, Camille and Sheryl, had more belief in me than I had in myself. They stood by my side through thick and thin, and I owe them my full and hearty gratitude. I am blessed to have their friendship and am grateful for their pushing me to write this book.

Most of all, I dedicate this book to all the great authors, past and present, who have given—and keep giving—their knowledge and skills to help motivate, inspire, and teach self-appreciation, motivation, and a positive outlook on everything, whether good or bad. These men and women paved the road for many of us seeking to get ahead in life and caused us to look deep inside ourselves and find the power we needed to achieve their goals. Without their books, I do not know where I would be today. Thank you to each and every author who has been an inspiration to me and given me the courage to write as well.

Introduction

Congratulations!

Your life is about to change—for the better.

This is the day that you have been waiting for, the day you begin to turn your life around, the day to turn yourself into the new you. What you are about to learn will make you feel good about who you are. Your future will look better, all because of a few changes in your everyday life.

You will be able to shop smart for the necessary items to achieve your goals. You will learn where to get quality, fashionable clothing at an affordable price. Every day will be a great day, because when you look into your closet, you'll find that you are able to coordinate your attire for the day with no problem at all. You will also be able to eliminate clothing, shoes, and accessories that take up space in your closet, because if you have not worn it in a year, you probably will never wear it again.

Gradually you will realize how much you can accomplish by being prepared at all times with your attire. You will save so much time on preparation, because you have the knowledge about what—and what not—to wear. Your confidence is a time saver.

While changing your attire is important, it's more important to get healthy and happy and have a great attitude. You will also learn how to change your diet and exercise and develop a positive attitude. When you stand back and look in the mirror, you'll be amazed at how your skin glows, how your hair shines, and how "together" you are. You will be proud of yourself and will develop an attitude that you can take on the world with full confidence and energy.

This is going to be exciting—not just for you, but for everyone who knows you. Let me be the first to congratulate you.

Start Dressing for Success

In Florida, where I live, it is fairly hot most of the year, so many of us feel we can get away with wearing a lot less. But this laid-back attitude can be unprofessional. We need to get back to the basics—class is "where it is at." This book is designed to help you develop a new attitude toward yourself and your business. You're making a statement to your clients, associates, family, and friends that you mean business—that you care about who you are and what you do. Your appearance in the business world can make or break you. A first impression is a lasting impression, so your initial contact with a client is extremely important. You should not dress offensively or be overdressed, gaudy, or loud. This book is meant to help you get back to the simple, basic dress for success that will help you in your business and help you feel better about yourself.

Years ago, people seemed to take more pride in how they looked. Even when they flew on an airplane, people got dressed up. I'm not suggesting that we go back to that more formal lifestyle, but at least we can be comfortable in a fashionable way. When you are in a business that deals with the public you could meet your next client—your next sale—on a plane, at a mall, or in a restaurant. If you are wearing baggy jeans, a big T-shirt, and flip-flops, you might not get that sale—just because of your appearance. Have you ever seen someone you have business dealings with in the grocery store or the mall and he or she is so sloppily or inappropriately dressed that you think, "Maybe I should consider doing business elsewhere?" Think about going to a doctor's office. It's clean, everyone is dressed professionally, and you feel good being there—you know the environment is appropriate. Imagine one day seeing your doctor at a mall or grocery store—anywhere except the beach—and he or she is dressed inappropriately and behaving poorly. You would most likely have second thoughts about continuing to see that doctor. Don't let someone have that kind of reaction to you. Let's get started helping you achieve your goal: dressing for success with a positive outlook on your future.

First things first. Start by looking in your closet. Are there more jeans than dress pants, more low-cut blouses than sharp-looking tailored ones? Are there any suits in your closet (winter ones as well as summer ones)? What types of dresses do you have? What types of skirts and pants do you wear? Are your clothes tight, wild, or out-of-date? Or do you have dresses and skirts in basic colors and tailored cuts? While most of these questions are geared more toward the women, men also have to take a good look in the mirror to see how others perceive them. If we become successful in our appearance first, our business success will come next. It is a challenge to change when everyone you know dresses a certain way, but professional people need to stand out and set an example that says, "We are professionals and this is how we dress." People are attracted to others who look knowledgeable and professional.

This book started out specifically for Florida realtors, but I realized that many of the messages apply equally to many professions and all climates. Replacing your wardrobe with more professional clothing can help all women and men.

The information in the book can certainly help anyone who desires change in all aspects of his or her life. Change can be difficult, but the desire can make the road to your goals easier. You can make these changes with very little money; in fact, you will have fewer items of clothing but will use each piece more effectively. As you change your appearance and attitude, the reactions of people to the "new you" may surprise you. My goal is to take you step by step through the process of determining what you should keep and what you need to get rid of. It's not going to be easy, but once you get started, it will get easier and more exciting. You will pride yourself on your first accomplishment, knowing that once you have purged certain items, you cannot wear them ever again. Your new motto is, "Out with the old and in with the new." Now let's get started!

For Girls Only

Stand in your closet, close your eyes, and envision how you want to look. Don't worry about the price. We can work on achieving this look in your price range. You can look like a movie star or model on any budget. Now open your eyes and look at what you have—what you wear and what you never wear. If you have not worn it in one year, you probably will never wear it again. Pull the items you really like and set them on your bed or couch (making sure they all fit you instead of wishing you were that size again). You need clothing for what's appropriate now, keeping in mind the profession you are pursuing. Styles change, and some of the items you really like may not be back in style for years to come. Remember, the goal is CHANGE and the time is NOW.

Good! You have started; you are on your way to the new you. Now look at what you have selected. Be honest; are the clothes in style? Are they in good shape? Do people see you wearing the same items over and over again? Not only is this boring for you, but it is also boring for people with whom you work or associate. You are a product of yourself; is that product questionable? If so, it is time to get rid of it. Start another pile on the floor in the bedroom of all the items you wear but really don't like (fat-day or rainy-day outfits—we will call them blue-day clothing). Also put in that pile your favorite items that you tend to wear too much.

The next step is to look at what is left in your closet—probably a lot more than you removed. Are you starting to see a dent in the closet or is it still overflowing with stuff you never wear?

Remember to keep in mind what you want to look like and how people will view you; the first impression is a lasting impression. You are dealing with the public! You are a professional! You want to look and act like a professional at all times (even in blue jeans). If you constantly think in these terms, it will become reality and you will automatically look fabulous and carry an air about you that attracts people to your business and gives you repeat business for years to come. Once you change the way you think, you will become that person and *a new you is born*.

Time to get back to the closet. Every item you never wear needs to go in another pile—even if it's a perfect color or an old favorite that you feel maybe one day you might wear again. Trust me, you never will. It has to go in the "bye-bye pile." Now put back on the racks what you have on the bed. We will add or subtract from this group. You should have at least three skirts for each season (one black, one gray, and one navy for the winter months, and tan, off-white, and brown for the fall). Another three for spring and summer—maybe white, charcoal black, and floral (only if floral looks good on you). If you are petite, you can also have flowing, soft pastel-color skirts; they always make you look sophisticated. Another important part of the skirt is its length. It should be in the middle of the knee cap or just below the knee cap, especially for short people. If you are tall, you can wear your skirts longer. If miniskirts, black leather, or wild, sexy slits are in fashion—they are not in fashion for your business.

Knee length has never gone out of style. Slacks are the next item you need. You'll need three for winter and fall, in black, gray, and navy, and three for summer—white, light gray, and charcoal black. Next are blouses. First of all, you need a bright white blouse. If your white blouses are yellowed or stained, get rid of them and invest in a crisp, new white blouse that fits comfortably. If you don't have them, buy a short-sleeve, a sleeveless, and a long-sleeve blouse *all in white*. Choose another five or six blouses in colors that look good on you. Please—no loud, low-cut, gaudy blouses. Remember, think like a professional. If you do not have these items, we will work on your budget. Make a note of items that you are missing.

Do you have any suits? As a realtor, you should have a black and a navy suit, preferably three-piece (skirt, slacks, and jacket). You cannot go wrong with suits. If you can afford it, get good brands that fit well. Nothing looks better than a man or a woman in a suit with a crisp white shirt or blouse, and high heels for the ladies and black dress shoes for the men. It's a great idea to go to consignment shops and buy very expensive, name-brand suits that would cost hundreds of dollars in the store. People who give away these suits usually only wear them once or twice. Consignment shops only take in clothing that is clean and in good condition, so you are getting quality at an affordable price. Do not feel belittled because you are buying at a consignment shop. Movie stars, millionaires, and successful people do not just throw these suits in the garbage when they are finished with them. You can have it dry-cleaned, and now you have a brand new, beautiful suit.

Those of you in warm climates should have a couple of pairs of capri pants with attractive sandals and summer cotton tops to wear when it is especially hot. Clients understand that this is acceptable due to the extreme weather. Remember to keep it looking professional and not overly casual. Have a couple of pairs of jeans, but don't wear them for meeting clients or showing homes unless you are in horse country; then it is appropriate.

As far as accessories, anything goes except huge earrings, nose rings, or items that make a political or controversial statement. You could lose a deal just by advertising your beliefs. Some people get offended or get a message that is totally the opposite of what you are trying to express. Bangle bracelets are very sophisticated, and pearl earrings are a must because they can be worn with anything. Shoes should be comfortable and not extremely high. I recommend two pairs of black heels (one patent leather for spring and summer, plus a simple pair of black leather). I also recommend a pair of red heels as well as tan or brown. There are so many nice sandals in the shops; you can stock up on these to mix and match. Can you see yourself right now dressed for success and looking good? People will notice, and men as well as women will want to do business with you.

Now that you are dressed as sharp as a pencil, let's talk about hair, makeup, hygiene, and perfumes. These are the touchy subjects, and a lot of you might not agree with me, but from my experience these are necessary subjects that must be spoken about.

As far as hygiene, one thing that could be offensive to others is when a woman meets them with greasy hair. There may be an odor to it, and it makes a statement that you are not taking care of yourself, so how can you take care of their business? Whether you have long or short hair, the most important thing to do is get a good haircut and keep it clean. That's all it takes. Another sensitive issue is bad breath. You can look like a million dollars, but if you have bad breath, no one is looking at your attire. They are trying to avoid your breath. This sounds harsh, but it is something that needs to be dealt with.

When it comes to makeup, less is best! Change is hard, but if you just try these techniques and find something that works for you and your skin color, you will be amazed at the results. A more natural look is more pleasing to clients than overdone, bold makeup is.

First things first. Buy a concealer that is just a shade lighter than your skin color. Put it under your eyes on dark circles as well as on sunspots (if you have any) or little marks on your face. Dab it on; do not rub it. Next, buy a sheer pressed powder and remember to always put it on in a downward stroke because you have tiny hairs on your face and they will stand up if you put it on in an upward stroke. All creams should be put on in an upward stroke, but not powder. The powder will make your skin even toned and not greasy. If you put makeup on in a warm climate like Florida's, it goes shiny and greasy once you step out in the heat; that is why pressed powder is the best. Once the powder is on, take a cotton ball or makeup sponge, dampen it and then dab it all over your face. This sets the powder, and you look natural all over.

Eyebrows are another subject. The best advice would be to go to a hair salon that has an expert in waxing or plucking the eyebrow. Each one of us has a unique shape to the brow that accents our eyes, making the eye a total package. If the brow has very little hair we can get an eyebrow pencil in the same shade as the brow. Put it on in the shape the brow goes (do not try to outline a differently shaped brow), and blend it in with a special brush that is made for the brow. This will make it look natural.

Next, we do the eyes in warm pastel shades for both eyeliner and eye shadow. Start with the shadow first. Use light to medium colors. Browns and light charcoal are good, and some blues and greens are okay—but do not use burgundy or bright greens or blues. They do not look natural at all. Some women look like geisha girls with all the bright, dark colors they put on their eyes. I am not putting geisha girls down, because I think they are beautifully made up in a style that is appropriate to their field—but not ours. Blend the eye shadow in an outward stroke and slightly up on the eye bone. Use a round eye shadow brush to blend it all in; you will find this a necessary tool. One good thing to do is to put a little white or beige color just under the eyebrows (blend it in of course); this makes the eyes appear wide open. Please, when we get to eyeliners, use a pencil and not liquid. You can blend your liner with a Q-tip so that it doesn't look like it's painted on.

Eyeliners should also be in browns or light charcoal. Dark black is a bold statement and is not natural unless you have naturally dark black hair. Let me be clear. You can be a little more extreme when you are on your own time than you can be when you are working. Again, blend the liner with a Q-tip into the eye shadow. The liner should be a little darker than the eye shadow, especially if you are using a brown eye shadow and a brown liner. One thing not to do is wear glittering eye shadows. They make a woman look older, and the look jumps out at a client. Of course, if you are younger, you can wear some glitter as long as it's not overwhelming.

Mascara completes the eye. Once your eye shadow and eyeliner are on, putting on mascara is your last and most important step. I recommend that you buy a really good mascara, one that does not clump up on your eyelashes, one that only needs one coat. It makes your lashes feel and look natural. Choose black or brown/black unless you are really blonde and fair, in which case you should use brown only.

Products Needed for Face and Eyes

- Powder makeup for people living in hot, humid climates
- Cream makeup if you have dry skin
- Warm color eye shadows
- White or beige eye shadow for under eyebrow
- Eyebrow pencil (if needed)
- Eyeliner in correct shade
- Cotton balls or makeup sponge
- Q-tips

- Special eyebrow brush
- Round eye shadow brush and sponge applicators
- Tweezers (if necessary)

Now we are getting to the blush and lips. Use a nice color blush that complements your face. A little can go a long way. Nothing looks worse than a woman who has a lot of blush on; when you see her all you see is cheeks. There are so many colors of blush that it is difficult for me to tell you which ones to get. If you have an olive skin tone, you can get away with a little darker color. If you have brown or black skin, you have to play around with colors that work for you. Women with fair skin should only wear light blush. When you buy a blush, be it powder or stick, always blend it in. Start at the hairline (not in the hair but the hairline) find your cheek bone and follow its lines along your cheek in a downward stroke. Blend it in with your fingertips so it does not look like a line of blush. If you use powder, buy yourself a good blush brush; when you put the powder on make sure you shake the excess powder off the brush before you put it on your face.

Last but not least is your lipstick. If you are young, you can outline your lips with a liner a little darker than your lipstick. Always put your lipstick on with a lip brush; it fills in any little cracks you might have and makes the lip look smooth and even. Older women can wear a liner as long as they don't try to make a line that isn't their natural lip line. Many women try to make their lips look full and plump by outlining the lip where there is no lip line. If your lips are very thin, there are ways to plump them up. Your lip liner and lipstick should be close to the same color, so that your lips are even toned and natural looking. Color is another issue. Please, no bright reds or burgundy. Use a subdued color to finish the whole natural picture. If you plan to put a glaze over the lips, just put it on the bottom lip. If you use it on both lips, once again, it is an eye-catcher and people will be staring at your shiny lips instead of listening to what you are telling them. Basically, find a style that accents your face and makes people take an interest in what you are saying and feel comfortable around you.

Please remember, everything I am suggesting you wear (clothing and makeup) is for the business world. When you dress up for an evening out, bright colors can be worn to match your outfit or the season.

When you shop for glasses, get a few opinions on your choices. I have a round face, so square eye glasses look best on me. Choose a color frame that accents your face. Don't get big glasses just because they are popular. Find something that never goes out of style. Glasses may seem like a little thing, but they have a big impact on your look.

As for cologne, go easy on it. Many people are highly allergic to perfume and find it offensive when you meet them and you reek of perfume. A small amount or none at all is best.

Products Needed to Finish the Face and Lips

- Blush in appropriate color
- Lip liner pencil in appropriate shade
- Lipstick
- Blusher brush
- Lip brush
- Glasses that suit your face

Now that you are complete, just remember—the sexy look is out of the picture for any professional career. If you are a woman realtor and show homes to a married couple in a sexy, low-cut outfit, more than likely, the man is looking at you and his wife is probably looking at her husband looking at you. It's usually the wife that makes the last decision about whether to buy or not, and she more than likely will look for another realtor just because she felt uncomfortable with you due to your attire. This is equally applicable to other careers in which you deal with both men and women.

Another important personal care item I have not yet mentioned is fingernails. They should be clean and a nice length. It does not matter if you wear false nails or your own. The important thing is that they are clean and have a nail polish that is not overly showy, like black or dark purple.

You are a total package now and you should feel proud of yourself. Wait until all your colleagues, friends, and family see you. You are going to look fabulous and want to buy something from yourself. Go for it, be the winner you are. I am proud of you for making a decision to change in order to feel better about yourself. This will help you in your business so you win in all avenues.

For Guys Only

There are many male realtors who are totally respected in the real estate business because they are considerate, honest, knowledgeable, happy people who can win anyone's trust. They take pride in their appearance, and they feel confident in themselves. Clients most likely will look at a realtor and think, *What do I see in this person? Does he take the time to understand what I am looking for? Does he listen or is he talking all the time? Is he dressed appropriately? Does he have knowledge about the home, piece of land, or commercial property I am interested in? If he does not seem to, I will start looking for someone else who is interested in what I am looking for, not what they* think *I am looking for.*

A man does not have to do a lot of work to look professional. Women have their makeup, their hair, and shoes that match the outfits. They have a lot more to do to get ready. Yet men can look so sloppy at times because they think completely differently from women. There is no problem with that, but when you are dealing with the public, there are rules that must be taken seriously to be successful in whatever profession you choose.

If a man does not know how to dress, he can learn. The first thing is properly fitting clothing. Measure your waist and your shoulders so that when you buy a suit, you will know what fits best. The best fit is comfortable—not too tight, but roomy and sharp looking. Clean-shaven is better than a beard or mustache. This is how the majority of today's businessmen look, yet some men are still living their lives in the sixties and seventies. Those days are gone. We are now in the twenty-first century and beards, mustaches, ponytails, and cowboy boots are not for the office unless you work in a field where they are accepted. You get the picture. Maybe it's just that no one has told you those days are gone. Please don't be offended. I am only suggesting that you make some changes to help you in your business.

When a man does not know how to dress, he needs to find a professional in this field to teach him, show him, and help him pick out some clothing. Just like women, once you get yourself dressed up, you will feel like a million dollars and you will know that you look sharp. The main thing is fit. If it fits, you will click with clients, family, and friends.

Some men's colognes smell better than women's colognes, but please don't overdo it. Sometimes it's hard to tell how much is too much. Start with two sprays, one on each side of the cheek. If you get compliments, then you know that it's perfect.

Make sure your shoes are clean, not dusty and marked-up, and please, please wear proper socks that coordinate with the suit or slacks (navy pants, navy socks; gray pants, gray socks). You know where I am going with this. Most important, please do not wear white socks unless your doctor tells you to (some people have a problem with color socks) or you are in a trade that requires them. White cotton socks are most comfortable when worn in steel-toed work boots. Construction workers need that because they are on their feet most of the day, outside in the heat. But if you wear a suit, white socks do not fit the outfit.

Another thing that is an absolute must for men is clean fingernails, cut to a proper length. No cigarette smoking when you are with clients. Even if you go to a restaurant, it might offend someone. Don't always talk to the men when you are working with a couple. Remember, the woman usually has the final say on most major purchases, so you must win her approval. Women notice how you dress and how you handle yourself.

Make sure you have clean teeth and nice-smelling breath. Nose hair, ear hair, and thick eyebrows should be trimmed. Please don't take offense, but it's like women with too much makeup. The person you are talking to only sees your flaws, and not the great, knowledgeable person that you are. Go to a good barber who can help you. There are small, handheld machines especially designed for that particular problem.

Florida is hot most of the time, so in my area, a nice, white, crisp shirt, slacks, black dress shoes and socks that match the pants are fine. Take your shirts to the cleaners, where they press them with expertise. Sometimes when it is extremely hot, a nice white cotton polo shirt is fine, depending on your profession. Most real estate agencies have a place where you can order shirts and have the company logo on them along with your name. This, too, is fine, as long as the colors are not too loud.

You need an attaché case for your business papers when you meet clients. Pens and paper should all go in the attaché case.

All the best to you in your new attire. Success is waiting for you around the corner.

What about Other Professions?

Okay, enough about realtors. This section is for TV announcers, CEOs, weather reporters, and anyone else who is in the public eye.

Watching the news on television is almost like watching a movie. Different styles of dress have overwhelmed television announcers. We see V-neck tops, outdated dresses, blouses with buttons ready to pop, and way-too-tight sweaters that show every detail of their undergarments. What in the world is happening here? Where has that professional appearance gone? Please have a little respect for yourself as well as the public. Years ago, when I worked for Petite Sophisticates, there was a news reporter that used to come into the shop and buy suits that fit her perfectly. She would ask our honest advice about how she looked and what type of shoe would go best with her outfit, even though most of the time, her feet were invisible while she was in front of the cameras. To her, it was important and she wanted to be complete. Her makeup was perfect and her hair was always neat. Even when she came into the store in blue jeans and a T-shirt, she looked fabulous, coordinated, and respectable. This is the way women and men in this field should always dress—presentable because they are in the public eye and we the public watch everything they do.

Yes, Florida is a laid-back state, but a professional is a professional. It's time for all of us to stand back and look at ourselves and how we dress. Do you walk out the door feeling ready for work? Do you feel confident that everything fits and is coordinated? Are you proud of your appearance and do you feel the public will feel the same way? Do you feel knowledgeable about your subject and totally prepared when the camera focuses on you? If you do not feel like this, then the public will feel the same way. Maybe you don't realize how the public regards you. Why not ask your coworkers for their honest opinions on what you are wearing that day? It might surprise you. A lot of people really do not see that they are dressed inappropriately until someone points it out to them. This goes for both women and men; it's not gender specific.

Some CEOs, weather and news reporters, and TV announcers are sharp—sharp dressers with sharp attitudes. They are a pleasure to look at and listen to. There are others who really need help. They probably do not realize that anything is wrong with how they look or act, so they continue to dress the same way. I feel the owners of the stations need to have a written dress code and a speaking skills class for all new employees. Employees that have been there for a long time need to have refresher courses. Television has changed over the years and continues to change with the times. New technology, high-tech computers, high-tech cell phones, and more are capable of doing almost anything. Monitors and televisions are getting bigger and better; they show everything, right or wrong, on an individual. If you work in front of a camera, you must always present yourself at your best, because you appear larger than life on some of these televisions. Your goal is to have the viewers come back to your station.

Whether you wanted to be a TV or radio announcer, a pilot, a doctor, or a candlestick maker, you would attach yourself to people in the profession you are interested in. You would ask questions, watch how they handle themselves, and pick their brain for any knowledge so you could become one of the elite, like they are. Questions you might ask yourself include, *Whom do I really respect in the business, and why is that person always getting ahead? To whom do I listen all the time when I am not the one in front of the camera?* Then ask yourself why you listen to and watch those people. How do they dress? Is their speech professional or are they all tongue tied? Then look at yourself and see if you are acting, dressing, and speaking like them. I respect your profession, but a lot of announcers are getting sloppy today. They look rough, they talk unprofessionally, and, to be honest, people would rather listen to someone who has it all together.

You may not like the things I have told you, but I just ask that you watch some other announcers, how they dress and present themselves. The other day, I was watching the news and the announcer had on a blouse that was cut so low that I felt if she bent down for any reason, there would be a "wardrobe malfunction"—an embarrassment for her as well as the station. I could not understand what she was trying to prove. I want to hear and watch the news, not a fashion show. If I watch a movie and actors are wearing clothing that fits the part, that's okay, even if it's outrageous, but when I am watching the news, my only interests are the weather where I live, the traffic, and the major events of the day. I do not want a fashion show. You are in the public eye; you don't have to be beautiful, you don't have to be slim, you don't have to have expensive clothing, but you do have to dress and act professionally and give viewers the news. What you do after hours is your business and honestly, that top you're wearing would be cute with a pair of jeans after hours, but it's not suitable for your profession.

Health, Exercise, and Just Plain Feeling Good

There are beautiful people that just glow with healthy skin, healthy hair, a complete package of health. You may ask yourself, Why wasn't I born to look healthy like them? What can I learn from what they are doing that will give me the same results that they have achieved? We all came into the world as perfect little people, with glowing skin and beauty shining through. Our parents took care of us with baths, lotions, shiny hair, and clean clothing, and we always, always smelled so good. The beautiful people have continued to do what their mothers and fathers did during their growing-up years. They take care of themselves—bathing, using lots of lotions, keeping shiny hair, and always smelling good. They exercise, eat good, nourishing food, and live healthy lives.

We all can change if we want to and look just like these healthy men and women. If you are overweight (and I have nothing against anyone overweight, but if you are not satisfied with your weight now, then do something about it), take action, get into eating nutritional foods, exercise, even if it is just a thirty-minute walk. The thing is, once you start exercising, all of a sudden you have more energy, your skin starts to glow, you feel healthy, and after a time your body will lose the weight it needs to. This in turn will make you feel better all over. Weight and size are just numbers. It's how you feel about yourself. Are you satisfied that you do not need to lose weight and feel good just as you are? Then I am sure it shows on the outside, so you will already have that natural glow. You will attract people to you automatically all because you know who you are. It shows in everything you do; this is what the public is looking for.

It's such a great feeling when your clothing starts to get too big and your friends and family remark on how great you look—all this just because you decided to take charge of your life. You are giving your body that healthy feeling and before you know it, your whole world changes. People start noticing you. You're still you, but a healthier, more energetic you.

You do not need to spend a lot of money to get yourself to this point in your life. One proven fact in losing weight is to count your calorie intake and portion your food. Carry a small notepad with you, and every time you put food or drink in your mouth, write down how many calories it contains. You will be very surprised when you add it up. Find out how many calories you should consume on a daily basis; some people are very active and need more than you might. You can find this information on the Internet or in some health or sports magazines. Cut out as much fat as you can. Butter and cheese are very high in fat, and sugar can also put on the pounds. Start to eliminate these foods little by little with healthier substitute foods that taste just as good without the harmful effects. It's the little changes at first, like taking your first cup of tea or coffee without sugar. As you start to do this, your coffee or tea will start to taste better without the sugar because you start to lose your desire for it. Eat fruit and vegetables. A doctor once told me if you eat a piece of fruit or a small salad with each meal, you will feel full all the time and it will benefit the body. If you want to be a healthy, slimmer person, these simple steps can put you in the right direction. Something amazing happens. You no longer desire these foods and you consciously know when you see them that they are not the better choice for your health.

These few changes in your life will start showing up on the outside as you are healing on the inside. I know you can do it. You will feel like a million dollars. It's really remarkable how so few changes in your life can help you. Please make sure you consult your doctor if you plan to change your eating habits. Some people may need to eat certain foods and stay away from others. If you have tried every diet, exercise and are still unable to lose weight, it might also be a good idea to ask your doctor to check out your thyroid with a simple blood test.

The reason I mention this is because I had an underactive thyroid. I never knew I had this problem but just could not lose the weight until the doctor recommend I get a thyroid test. If you are given proper medication for your thyroid, you will no longer feel tired, and if it's an underactive thyroid, this could be one of the causes of your weight. We all should be thankful for the Internet, because we can investigate any diagnosis a doctor might give us. We can read up on it and get to know exactly what is going on in our bodies.

When it comes to exercise, you do not need to spend money on a gym or gym equipment. This can become costly. There are so many ways to exercise. Walking is one of the best exercises you can do. You do not need to do it alone; go with your spouse, a friend, a relative, or one of the kids. Pace yourself slowly at first, and then, as time goes on, you will be able to speed it up and burn more calories. You should do at least thirty minutes a day. The more you do, the more calories you burn. Make sure you are dressed properly with comfortable clothing appropriate to the weather. Most of all, you have to have a good pair of walking shoes. If you're going to invest money in your exercise program, the number one item to buy is walking shoes; it will be worth it in the long run.

If you can afford a treadmill for your home, it's great for those rainy days. You can sometimes pick them up at a garage sale at an amazing price. Check EBay or Craigslist; you can usually find one at a very low price. You can also join the YMCA; it's much cheaper than other gyms. They have a family plan so you can take the kids at an affordable price. They have swimming pools as well as all the gym equipment you could possibly want.

You should lift weights when you are dieting. When we lose weight, our muscles can become weak and saggy, so building muscle is important. You should start lifting weights slowly; start with small barbells or arm weights; they cost between five and ten dollars and you can get them at your local drugstore. If money is a challenge in the beginning, then get a couple of cans of peas or corn which weigh about a pound. Progress to larger cans as you gain strength.

If you have not been exercising for a long time, take it slowly at first and build up to a faster pace. Again, make sure to speak with your doctor first and let him know what you are planning to do. Most doctors are delighted if you start walking. Swimming is one exercise that works out your whole body and is easier on your muscles. During the summer months, you can find me swimming in the pool. If you like the water, swim as much as you can. Join the YMCA just for the joy of the swimming pools. As I mentioned previously, swimming is an exercise that uses every part of your body; it's an allover weight program by itself. If you live up north, swim in the summer and cross-country ski in the winter months. Cross-country skiing is also an allover weight program. The main thing is you must do some form of exercise to reap the benefits.

At first you might think, *Where will I find the time to do this*? You will be amazed at how much time you will have. You can get away from the negative news on the television and enjoy some time for your body—and possibly enjoy that time with your spouse and kids as well. Once you start doing this, you will make sure you have the time, because you're going to feel like a million dollars. You will look fabulous and feel healthy, and, believe me, you will have better skin, better nails, and beautiful, shiny hair. Get up and start walking; it does the body good.

The greatest thing about exercise and taking care of your health is that this is the first steps to change. Once you get started, once you see the results, you will begin to take other steps to change. One of them will be to clean out your closet to eliminate what you don't want and refill it with what you need—probably in a smaller size.

Who I Am

My name is Colleen Craddock. I have lived in Fort Lauderdale and Stuart, Florida for more than thirty years. I am a make-up artist, certified color analyst, and interior decorator. I have a degree in fashion merchandising, and presently my field is real estate. Most of my life has been dedicated to helping people, taking the time to listen to their needs and/or the challenges they may be experiencing in their lives, especially if they are just getting started in their first jobs. Sometimes all people need is to have someone to listen to them. More than likely they will solve their problems on their own. It's tough out there when you are just getting started and all you want is some advice on how to get off on the right foot.

I explain to people that what worked for me over the years may not work for them in today's world. It is very interesting to study how people carry themselves, how they speak, and how they dress. My experience has led me to some of the most amazing people; they may be models, professional singers, doctors, lawyers, painters, builders, or pilots—all walks of life. I have learned from each of them and feel honored to have had them in my life. There were times I would do some fashion shows for the working professionals and wannabe professionals. One of my businesses was called "Beauty and You." It was all about *you*. Another business was called "Just between Friends—Add Memories and Stir." A friend of mine and I opened the shop. We had people keep a log of some of the special moments they had with their friends. It was great while it lasted—people love to talk about themselves—but it was too short-lived. We had something going that could have been another book all on its own. People still ask me about the shop.

One thing I know for sure, people will always need some type of advice. I hope you take the time to listen to them; it will leave you feeling good and them feeling great that someone took the time to listen to them. Helping someone always helps you. I take pride in myself and in my dress; people used to say, "Colleen, even when you are bumming around, you are always appropriately dressed." I get that in the real estate business as well, and I know I keep myself aware of my attitude and appearance. It's all up to you; people can make themselves miserable, or they can make themselves feel good. I choose to have a good outlook and be happy and strive for as much perfection as I can. Positive people always win; first they win because people who are happy live longer. There have been studies on that and it's true whatever field people are in. There are days when I wake up on the wrong side of the bed and my attitude is not what it should be. I have to snap out of it, because it will totally ruin my day and keep people away from me, and I will wallow in my misery all by myself. I don't want to make myself miserable and have my friends, coworkers, and family wonder what in the heck is wrong with me. I choose to make my world as peaceful as I can, and happiness is my number one key.

When I was growing up, my family was very poor. We were on welfare, so we had to live wherever the city put us, and that was in the slums of Toronto. Many times we went without food; we never dressed well and wore clothing that we received from other people or the Salvation Army. I was skinny and sick a lot. All the other children around me were as poor as I was, so I never knew there was a different lifestyle I could have. I didn't understand that this life I was living was not normal. I honestly believed that this was how everyone lived, but once we moved from our wartime home to the city of Toronto, life was so different that I couldn't believe my eyes. There were high-rise buildings, streetcars, and beautiful people everywhere dressed in stylish outfits. I thought, *Wow! Where have I been all my life?* At first, I was laughed at and pushed around in school. The kids mocked me because I was skinny, dressed funny, and was not as smart as they were (at least that's what they thought). I never got angry at them, because they didn't know who I was. They had no idea that my upbringing was so different from theirs, so I understood that they didn't understand. These children grew up with both a mom and a dad, lived in one home all their lives, and never went without food or nice clothing, but I must tell you that they changed my attitude toward life. They gave me a burning desire to prove myself and to be the best I could be in the circumstances I lived in. These children helped me change my direction and desires in life to become the person I am today. They will never know how much they played a part in all the great things I have done.

I decided to change my life right then and there. I was not going to allow people to control my attitude anymore, so I went to the library and started reading about people that made it in life, people that started their lives like me, with very little, but chose to overcome their beginnings and proceed to a completely different lifestyle. No one laughed at me anymore. My appearance changed, my attitude was different, and I took an interest in everyone I met. People noticed that I was different, I had goals and ambitions, and I was out to make them happen. I started babysitting. With the money, I bought myself some nice clothing, invested in some good shoes, and fixed up my hair. It didn't matter what anyone else thought about me; it mattered that I felt good about myself.

Downtown Toronto is where the elite and well-dressed people spend their time. They eat at high-class restaurants, buy beautiful clothing in the larger department stores, attend the theaters, get their hair and nails done, and smile a lot. I knew that would be me one day because I wanted to be a part of that life, so whenever I got the chance to go to Toronto, I went. I spent hours and hours walking and sitting outside these restaurants, theaters, and department stores, just so I could watch the people—how they walked, how they dressed, what they talked about, what they ate, and where they were going. I knew by watching and listening to them I could understand how they got this lifestyle, which would teach me the next steps I needed to take to achieve my own goals. It's like putting a puzzle together; all the pieces start to fit. When you want something badly enough, you seek out whatever avenues you need to take to achieve your goals. My goal was to better myself, so just observing people in their everyday tasks was a start for me. Slowly I started moving forward and my life began to take shape. I was molding myself into the person I wanted to be.

I met a woman in Toronto at Vic Tanny's gym. She was a former model and absolutely beautiful. She took an interest in me; she told me I was special and pretty. No one had ever told me I was pretty before. She taught me about life, she made me feel beautiful (even though I was sickly and skinny), she challenged me to look deeper in myself to seek what I wanted to do with my life, and she told me to see what other people saw in me. Little by little, I started to change. I started putting on a little weight, which gave me a shape and gave me confidence. I looked in the mirror and saw a different person. I saw someone I liked and was craving more and more knowledge about attitude. I do not remember the name of my model friend, but she really is the one that set the path for me to find myself, and

I began learning about me and what my opportunities were. I want to thank her from the bottom of my heart.

Today I still crave knowledge. I read all the time, mostly books that lift me up, books that help me stay up to date and knowledgeable in today's high-tech world. You have to keep up with today's society so you don't get left behind. I also take classes on specific subjects that interest me. I have added so much to my life and have met so many friends along the way. I like who I am and I want the same thing for you. If you are struggling, I know where you are and I know how you feel, because I was there. You can become whatever you want to be, because you are a child of God and he wants what is best for you. Get up, dust yourself off, and take the first step to finding out how beautiful you truly are. I believe in you, even though I do not personally know you. I was where you are at; I was you, so if I can change, so can you. Wash your face, get dressed, and get to a library. It's a good starting place for anyone.

The Attitude of a Winner

Be what you wish, but I choose to be a winner—no in between, no cover up. I am a winner in all aspects of my life because I have taken control of my attitude. You, too, can be a winner if you choose to. It's all up to you—no one else, just you. Take control of your attitude. You ask, "How do I do that? You don't understand my situation! You can't possibly think I can be a winner when so much is happening in my life. Please tell me how I can be positive all the time, during my hardship, during my sorrows, during my particular situation. What makes you different from me?" Well, sit down, get a good cup of coffee or tea, and listen seriously to what I am about to say.

Start reading books on positive thinking, books that teach you how to become a winner, books that teach you how to get rid of the "stinking thinking." Change your attitude and prepare yourself for success. It's all based on the actions you take. Once you realize your potential and believe you can become anything you put your mind to, it's the beginning of your journey to the new you. The books will teach you how to handle your situations and challenges with your attitude toward them. Trust me, it works. I know because I once was exactly where you are now!

I must admit that sometimes I get depressed and feel lonely, but it does not last long because I have learned how to snap out of it. I begin to analyze what is happening at that particular time, dissecting it and trying to find out what brought the feelings on in the first place. I know there is a reason this is happening and, from past experience, I know a good outcome will result from my analyzing. The good outcome could be simply a lesson learned from dealing with the situation, which then helps me to deal with similar problems. But the good outcome could also be that my experience enables me to be of assistance to others who may find themselves facing the same challenge. I have experienced the privilege of helping others many times, based on my having had the same challenges. This is part of my motivation for writing this book.

When I face a challenge in my life the very first thing I do is pray. I am not saying that is what you should do, but I have a comfort zone that allows me to speak openly to my maker and know I will not be judged or ridiculed. I seem to always get an answer in one way or another. Everyone in the universe has to have a place to go to vent, to ask questions, to try and understand what is happening. For me, I go to my comfort zone and find peace in my faith. I always come away relieved, with a whole new attitude about what I am doing wrong and a plan to make it right. You have to find that special place for yourself.

I choose to read positive thinking books because we live in such a negative world. When do you ever hear good news from radio or television announcers? They thrive on the negative and will capitalize on bad news for weeks at a time. We are inundated with negative statements and thoughts. Is it any wonder that we so often feel depressed, upset, negative, and unmotivated and cannot understand our moods? I do not blame the announcers; this is their job.

You can deal with this by erasing it from your mind, simply replacing it with positive thoughts and information. Turn off the news, pick up a positive book that will tell you how great you really are and make you believe that you have the ability to become whatever you desire. Success is not based on color, shape, size, mentality, family background, or education. It is simply based on believing in yourself and knowing we have all been given the same qualities to become whatever we want to become.

It may be that no one has told you that before; no one has taught you how to clean out your mind of the stinking thinking and put power in your thoughts. Good thoughts lead to good results. If you want to become something in life or act like people you admire, then you must associate with people that have the qualities you would like to see in yourself. Talk with them and consume their knowledge about how and why they achieved their success. Sometimes it can be difficult to have access to these successful individuals, but they are in the books and on your television and radio. Some of these successful people want to help you and have written positive books themselves explaining how they got to where they are today.

I will provide you with a list of different books to read—ones that I have read that helped me believe in myself. I have had some difficult experiences in my life and had to learn to get rid of all the negative thoughts so I could move forward, pick myself up, dust myself off, and start all over again in the right direction. They helped me to learn that by creating a positive atmosphere for myself, I could hurdle over those obstacles that come my way so that I can be the winner that I choose to be.

I sincerely hope that this book is able to help anyone who is facing challenges and having to cope with problems in today's society, but don't limit yourself to my book. It could be any one of the positive thinking books that are readily available, even through our public libraries.

Once you clear your mind and can see that there is a way for you to succeed, take the next step and you will be amazed at what will take place. If you need to go back to school in order to reach your career goals, your attitude will help you with the desire and resources you need to do this. By going back to school, you will meet other individuals who have the same interests you have and this will motivate you to continue. It's all baby steps that get you there; once you get started, it will all flow into place.

Everyone in the world is special. We are all blessed to be born in this big, beautiful world. From the time we are conceived to the time of our births, miracles are taking placed in our minds and bodies. It doesn't matter where we were born; we have all come into the world the same way. If you have the same interest as someone from China, Pakistan, Africa, England, Canada, Italy—anywhere in the world—there is automatically a special bond between all of you (even though you cannot understand each other's language). You know where their heart is; they think like you, they want what you want; they are working toward their goals just as you are.

Books to Help You Get There

The very first book I read was called *University of Success*, by Og Mandino. I still read this torn-up, battered book today. Every time I read it, I pick up something positively new. This is one of the reasons I decided to write my book.

My favorite author is Zig Ziglar. In one of his books, *Top Performance*, he comments, "Remember, you find what you look for in life." He goes on to explain that no matter where he goes—New York, California, anywhere in the world—he can find negative, objectionable people involved in drugs and crime, or he can find beautiful, loving, caring, dedicated, God-fearing, flag-waving, family-loving people. It just depends on what you are looking for. You will *find* what you are looking for.

Frank Bettger wrote *How I Raised Myself from Failure to Success in Selling*. Among other things, he writes about how successful men should look: "Put yourself in the hands of an expert, he'll teach you how to dress. Don't look like a football player if you're trying to be successful in business." If you want to be a businessman, then you must look like one. Get a good haircut; learn how to tie a tie, *look your best*. If you don't know how to do it, put yourself in the hands of an expert. This also goes for women. Start looking and acting like a business woman. Stop trying to look like you are going to a party; start looking like a professional.

In *Wake Up and Dream*, Pat Mesiti writes, "It doesn't matter where you've been in life. What matters is where you're going." Everybody gets hurt; everybody has disappointments. Hurt is hurt and failure is failure, no matter how it's packaged. How you respond to it makes all the difference in the world. If you live in the ghetto, don't let the ghetto live in you—do something about it. Dream big dreams; if your dreams are too small, you won't be motivated to grow.

Another great author is Doug Hooper. One of his books is called *You Are What You Think*, and it's a powerful book. Hooper writes, "The only thing necessary to effect a change in a person's life is *Desire for Change*." Ralph Waldo Emerson said, "Do the thing and you will *have* the power." Remember that quote the next time an opportunity presents itself. Emerson continues, "If you look back and realize you have made mistakes, do not be resentful and full of self-condemnation. Instead be grateful that you will have opportunities to learn and profit from these mistakes."

In Tim Connor's *The Road to Happiness Is Full of Potholes*, he writes, "People are looking for the big "Potholes" in the jungle trail that will wipe them out. Reality check … Elephants don't bite, but you can die from a mosquito bite. Lesson Learned: 'The neglected, the simple, the little things will get you every time.'" What are your potholes? Those little things that are holding you back. They are the cannots, should haves, I'll nevers, or *I'm not educated enough, I don't look the part, I'm not smart enough*. These are serious setbacks in your life. Cut it out and replace them with can, will, always, knowing, studying, and a burning desire to achieve your goals. You are your own worst enemy. Stop beating yourself up; do something about it. You can become whatever you want. Believe in yourself. God gave you a brain like He did everyone else and you do have a purpose in life, so the self-pity party stops here.

Robert Schuller and Dale Carnegie are my teachers. These men helped shape and mold me into who I am today. Words could never express my gratitude toward them. I do not know how many times I have read their books; I still reread them today. Their words will jump out at you, make you say, "Oh, yes. That is true; are they writing about me?" Both men are straightforward in their writing. Most of all, they want you to be happy and prosperous—not just financially, but in everyday life. God gave these men an understanding of all mankind.

I have a little story to tell about Robert Schuller. I watched him on TV many years ago, when I was really trying to find myself and deal with the many difficult experiences I was having. One of them I had a hard time getting over—it was that I was molested when I was a child. Many years went by and I found that there was a roadblock relating to my past experience that kept holding me back. I had never told anyone about what had happened to me, so I was carrying it around for years. Then one day I was watching Robert Schuller and he said, "Someone out there is hurting real bad. Just pick up the phone and talk to one of the counselors, because God loves you, and so do I."

I called and poured my heart out to a perfect stranger, and amazingly, I began to release a lot of my feelings. This helped me feel better about myself. The counselor told me about some books to read and told me it was not my fault. A few weeks later, I got a letter from Dr. Schuller. He wrote a phrase in that letter that I will never forget, and I still live by it today: "Lift yourself up and soar with the eagles, because you are a gift from God." I realized that what I went through helped prepare me to deal with life situations. As a result, I have been able to help others who have had similar experiences. When I have repeated the advice I received from Dr. Schuller, it has help them as well.

If you are having emotions that are holding you back, you can overcome them. Expect miracles to happen and they will. You are already setting new paths just by reading this book. You're on the right track and I am proud of you. If you think about it, you are already a miracle. You came into this world with a brain, fingers, toes, eyes, a mouth, a nose, and all the other parts. The body is a masterpiece all on its own. You're a *miracle*, as is everyone else in the world—amazing, isn't it.

Dale Carnegie is the author of all self-help authors. He started the whole positive-thinking ball rolling with *How to Win Friends and Influence People.* He wrote another book, *How to Stop Worrying and Start Living.* This book may help improve your health and add years to your life, because worry can make you sick. In the book, Carnegie tells us that worry saps our energy, warps our thinking, and kills ambition. Something can be done about this with practical formulas that can be put to work and last a lifetime. As I mentioned before, read positive-thinking books. They may save your life.

I have saved the best for last: *The Secret* by Rhonda Byrne. Before I get into it, I need to tell you about my brother, because I believe this book gave him more time than we expected. I went to Toronto, Canada, because my brother was seriously sick. He had had some surgery and was never the same after that. He was hospitalized for ten months before the Lord took him home. I went to spend as much time as I could with him. I was there for one week, and every day I went to see him in the morning and stayed until the evening. He wasn't really there with me mentally, but my friend gave me *The Secret* to read when my brother was asleep. The book made so much sense to me and helped me deal with my brother's situation. (Special thanks to my friend Sheryl for lending me the book.) As I started reading it, I started to get excited about what it was saying. I started reading it to my brother and he became more coherent to me; he started to know who I was and he would smile a little and hold my hand. I read him one of the stories from the book, about a man named Morris Goodman, who was in a plane crash and was completely paralyzed. His spinal cord was crushed, his first and second cervical vertebrae were broken, and his swallowing reflex was destroyed. He could not eat or drink. His diaphragm was destroyed so he couldn't breathe. All he could do was blink his eyes. He was told he would be a vegetable the rest of his life. But he told himself that he had his mind and he would not believe he was going to remain like that. He was on a respirator and they said he would never breathe on his own again, but a little voice inside said, "Breathe deeply, breathe deeply." Finally, he was weaned from the respirator. He set goals for himself, and today Mr. Goodman is living proof that "man becomes what he thinks about." He now speaks around the world and writes about his experience.

I went to Toronto expecting to see my brother days before he was supposed to die, but I believe my reading this story to him helped him to start coming around. I saw the change in one week. When I left, I felt good. He lived a few months after that, but everyone told me he had changed. He was funny again, like he used to be. I believe this story kept him living a little longer and in better spirits. He died, but I do know he was happier than when I first saw him. By the way, it was my brother who encouraged me to read my first positive-thinking book. He read all kinds of books, most of them on positive thinking. I believe this got him through life and he was able to cope with anything that came his way. When I visited, I was staying at his home. I noticed he had a copy of *The Secret* but he had not read it yet. I guess I was supposed to be there to read the book to him.

I am telling you this because I want you to feel your best at all times, and reading positive books will help you throughout your life. If you are constantly negative, then you are only going to attract negativity, which will make you miserable and unmotivated all the time. One phrase I hear a lot is, "Bad things happen to me all the time." If you find yourself saying this, *stop now*! Because when you are thinking this all the time, it's going to bring bad things into your life. Even if you do not understand this, try something for me as well as for yourself: *Think only positive thoughts*. Start with something small. Believe a good friend you have not seen or heard from in a long time, someone with whom you once experienced fun and good times, will call you. Keep thinking this and believing that your friend will call. It will happen. Maybe not today, but out of the blue one day, that friend will call. Just try it; you will be surprised. This little test could be the start of a change in your thinking, which in turn will improve your life.

I believe this book will be a new beginning for you. I would love to hear from some of you regarding how your life has changed. Take pictures of you now, and once you get yourself beautified and start thinking good thoughts about who you are, take another picture. You will be amazed how beautiful you look as well as how you feel. My e-mail address is cscrealtor@comcast.net, and I would love to hear from you. Now it's all up to you, so get up, get ready, and start living your life. It's going to be a blast, full of fun, excitement, and dream building. I'll be by your side all the way. *Go show the world what you are all about!*

Things to Remember

* *Always find the good in people. Everyone has special qualities.*

* *Believe in yourself—you are very special.*

* *You are who you think you are—so think good thoughts.*

* *Stay positive, even when you think it can't get any worse.*

* *Show the world what you are made of. Put your best foot forward and keep going.*

* *Find your purpose in life.*

* *Step out of your comfort zone.*

* *Try, try, try—until you succeed!*